My Life as a Doll

My Life as a Doll

Elizabeth Kirschner

Autumn House
Press

PITTSBURGH

Autumn House Press Staff
Executive Editor and Founder: Michael Simms
Executive Director: Richard St. John
Community Outreach Director: Michael Wurster
Co-Director: Eva-Maria Simms
Fiction Editor: Sharon Dilworth
Special Projects Coordinator: Joshua Storey
Associate Editors: Anna Catone, Laurie Mansell Reich
Assistant Editor: Courtney Lang
Editorial Consultant: Ziggy Edwards
Media Consultant: Jan Beatty
Tech Crew Chief: Michael Milberger
Administrator: Rebecca Clever
Volunteer: Jamie Phillips

ISBN: 978-1-932870-20-6
Library of Congress Control Number: 2007943444

All Autumn House books are printed on acid-free paper and meet the international standards of permanent books intended for purchase by libraries.

This project was supported by the Pennsylvania Council on the Arts, a state agency, through its regional arts funding partnership, Pennsylvania Partners in the Arts (PPA). State government funding comes through an annual appropriation by Pennsylvania's General Assembly. PPA is administered in Allegheny County by Greater Pittsburgh Arts Council.

for Susan

The Autumn House Poetry Series

Michael Simms, Executive Editor

Snow White Horses, Selected Poems 1973–88 by Ed Ochester

The Leaving, New and Selected Poems by Sue Ellen Thompson

Dirt by Jo McDougall

Fire in the Orchard by Gary Margolis

Just Once, New and Previous Poems by Samuel Hazo

The White Calf Kicks by Deborah Slicer
● 2003, selected by Naomi Shihab Nye

The Divine Salt by Peter Blair

The Dark Takes Aim by Julie Suk

Satisfied with Havoc by Jo McDougall

Half Lives by Richard Jackson

Not God After All by Gerald Stern
(with drawings by Sheba Sharrow)

Dear Good Naked Morning
by Ruth L. Schwartz ● 2004,
selected by Alicia Ostriker

A Flight to Elsewhere by Samuel Hazo

Collected Poems by Patricia Dobler

The Autumn House Anthology of Contemporary American Poetry,
edited by Sue Ellen Thompson

Déjà Vu Diner by Leonard Gontarek

Lucky Wreck by Ada Limon ● 2005,
selected by Jean Valentine

The Golden Hour by Sue Ellen Thompson

Woman in the Painting
by Andrea Hollander Budy

Joyful Noise: An Anthology of American Spiritual Poetry, edited by Robert Strong

No Sweeter Fat by Nancy Pagh ● 2006,
selected by Tim Seibles

Unreconstructed: Poems Selected and New
by Ed Ochester

Rabbis of the Air by Philip Terman

Let It Be a Dark Roux: New and Selected Poems by Sheryl St. Germain

Dixmont by Rick Campbell

The River Is Rising by Patricia Jabbeh Wesley

The Dark Opens by Miriam Levine ● 2007,
selected by Mark Doty

My Life as a Doll by Elizabeth Kirschner

● winner of the annual Autumn House Press
Poetry Prize

Acknowledgments

Many thanks to Susana Roberts, Wendy
Mnookin, Mimi White, and Leslie Ullman for
their careful, caring readings of these poems.

"The Lock-Up" has been published in
nth position.

Contents

1 • Cuckoo

Why do I love the winter garden so?
Is it because I hear the dirge

of dirt, elegy of vanquished blossoms?
Whatever emerges at season's end

comes from a harrowing heaven: yesterday,
I believed I was a wooden woman

with a wooden heart the wolves
would tear apart. I jerked

about like a marionette with
tangled strings—slash of claws, teeth

sinking in to rip the flesh off
my wooden bones. When I was four

years old, my mother pummeled
the back of my head with a baseball bat.

I remember the pain. I remember
hitting the floor like a scarecrow

that was a heap of broken straw.
This is why I love the winter garden so:

energy of enigma. Icy blossoms.

After my mother hit the back
      of my head with the bat's
            sweet spot, light cried

its way out of my body.
      I could not yet tie my own
            shoes. I could not yet pour

my own milk, but deeply
      down and down I went
            like a ball bouncing down

the cellar stairs. There
      I played with my dolls.
            They kept their conversations

to themselves, talking
      behind my back.
            I was one of them—

a doll carved out of a dog's
      bones, molded from stone,
            or torn-up twisted rags.

As in all the dolls, my heart
      was a single drop of blood
            pulsing like a tiny red spider

trapped in its own lair:
      the web of my making
            is the web of my undoing.

My soul was scant—
      a grain of salt burning
            like an ember under the tongue.

My life as a doll
     was a life of waiting—hours
          reeled like pinwheels, days

passed like wind blown
     through black holes, weeks
          hung heavy as headstones.

Then God took a knife
     cut me into pure pain,
          alive amid birds

wilding in the grapevine
     while my dreams angled
          into me like hooks, dragging me

away from Mother
     into a world
          he forgot to bless.

A divinity of demons
called me by name:
Elizabeth, Elizabeth.
I sleepwalked on the sea at night
dreaming of sinking into molecules
of water that muscled me under
relentless tides.
Swish, swish
went my soul,
that tiny anchor,
size of a thumbnail.
Ship ahoy! I cried,
ship ahoy!
but my dreams
streamed out of me
in dribbles and scribbles of air:
to be me was to be
an ounce of darkness
sucked into the moon's
dead gut.
Blip, blip went my heart
that wanted to be tossed
like a copper penny
in a wishing well:
I wanted a new mother
whose flesh would be
soft and warm, inviting
while my real mother
wore a mask cracked and caked
with the dust I so willingly
wanted to become:
salvation was a hardship
I was not yet ready to bear.

On the day I ran away
the light felt bullied.
I packed my pink suitcase
embossed with a kitten
and took off into the woods
surrounding the house.

The summer birds followed me.
I was camouflaged by the tender
undersides of leaves. I wanted
to live in a fairy house,
knew one awaited me
somewhere in the woods.

I held my hand out in order
to catch spindrift seed, knowing
if I caught just one it would burst
into a magic flower. This flower
would speak to me. This flower
would know there was a secret
blue butterfly trapped inside
the prison house of my bones.

When Mother found me,
she beat me until my marrow
ran cold, until the air
raped me. I long
to face her now. I long
for her to eat my tears which
have turned to glass splinters.

Let them slice, slice, slice
her dead tongue until her dead
words are bubbles of blood
while her skeleton's corpse wanders—
lost, homeless, hungry—
in the scarred woods.

At night, I danced before
my bedroom mirror. I wore

a flannel nightgown with snowmen
on it all year round. I was

a dancing specter. I believed
I could squish my brains out

by pressing on the side of my head with
the palms of my hands. *Your body*

is a temple, said the nun at school,

but she whacked my hand with a ruler,
and Mother struck my head with a bat—

I twirled and twirled. I
made tiny leaps: my limbs

were lithe in the already decaying
temple of my body, my heart,

a cup of leftover light, tippily,
toppily turned upside down.

I gathered twigs to make
a twig house my mother
couldn't blow down.
Her breath came from a fugitive demon
and I was her fugitive girl.
Twig upon twig,
twig upon twig,
house or funeral pyre?
My soul slowly burned
and my heart was a hollow stone
buried within the graveyard
of my body.
I could say winter
turned my bones
into splintered icicles,
but I was stillborn,
one who knew birth and death
are two faces,
an unlucky coin.
Toss me up, toss me down,
toss me round and round
while my numb words
fill my numb head: eat
your breath, spit out your blood
till God tucks you in his
empty pockets, a God
so frightened he hides
in heaven's jail.
Give me the latchkey
for I'm the little match girl
whose vivid hallucinations are
so beautiful God cries
and cries for more.

One year I won a turtle
in the turtle race at the school's
Fun Fair. I took it home
in a little cardboard box that
looked like it was meant to carry
Chinese food. I set up
the turtle tank. It had
a little island in it,
a blue umbrella.

That night, Mother,
boozed up, hit the hallway walls,
like a sack of potatoes. I held
my turtle to my breast, as though
it were a green rose.

My eyes sank into their sockets.
Marrow evaporated from my bones.
Who could save me while
the purple poodles on my wallpaper
became rabid?

If I thought hard enough
would the restless angels descend
to mother the missing person
I was—I longed
to have my picture on the back
of milk cartons at school—
while my real mother sleep-
walked in my crucified shadow?

*   .

In my playhouse in the woods, I baked tea cakes for my
Patty Play Pal

whose eyes were ogled marbles, whose limbs were molded
by a God

wise because he was speechless.
I wanted

to wear lipstick the color of blood, high heels
and cocktail dresses,

but my mind was attacked by a hurricane of birds. Feathers,
feathers everywhere.

Bits of my flesh rained down from ravenous clouds.
I practiced dying,

emulated the dark particles hulled by demons which burst
like tiny explosions…

poof, poof, poof, was how I got myself out of
this world—

I longed to sleep the dream of apples hung in ornate orchards where
blooming and dying

were one and the same thing. *Think thing*, I thought,
think thing,

because Patty was a thing and I knew not what to do to be
a bit of an it

while birds descended like flames and I burned down inside
my playhouse,

a relic in a bed of ash,
a secret

only my doll knew about, but her lips, like God's,
were sealed.

I was a cuckoo girl who lived
in a cuckoo house whose walls
trembled and cracked.
I wore a poisonous bee dress
to ward off my mother.
If she touched me,
she would be stung by
one hundred thousand bees.
Buzz, buzz
went the spring air.
Ding-dong
went the bell in my hell.
At night, I heard the stars'
roaring voices:
go forward into your netherland until

…until I was nothing more than
    a stillborn hint
        on absent air.

When Mother came after me, I put
    a book or a pot lid down my pants
        to soften the blows. This, too:

I hid Dixie cups full of violets
    in the kitchen cupboard
        for her to find and penny candy tucked

into the mailbox with the mail.
    I used to hide inside the cellar's
        crawl space where Mother

could not find me. I read
    "The Little Match Girl" by flashlight
        over and over because I was

that freezing girl in a frozen world
    whose hallucinations soothed her.
        I carried a bouquet of burnt

matches. I sang lullabies
    to myself while my heart,
        a knotted bone, froze.

Before sleep could arrive
like a caress, I wanted to
muzzle the purple poodles
on my wallpaper, rip

out claws while my room
rocked back and forth. It grew
large, then small and there was
no mother I could cry out to.

The purple poodles growled, showed
their teeth. The moon cracked
like a blue egg and the star-tree
shattered its own blossoms.

Dear God, where were you?
Were you comforting the mothers
of the war dead? Only you
could have turned me back

into a girl who, come morning,
would cup the shattered blossoms
while her stone hands and
stone lips slowly softened.

In my second grade classroom,
I listened to particles of light burst open.

Each made a little *ping* sound and
blinked on and off in swirls of breathless dust.

I knew the light was alive. *Ping, ping, ping*—
I wanted everyone to hear the light sing.

Instead, the priest came in: his face
looked cloudy and botched, but his words

scourged me: *because of your sins you will*

burn in the pits of hell. This was when

my demons first came to me: hooking me
with claws, carrying me home.

I went into the windowless bathroom without
turning on the light. I sat down on the toilet

knowing my sins were needles, were daggers,
murderous with their might. Slowly,

carefully, I unwound the toilet paper, placed
a piece on my head like a chapel veil.

I used the rest to wipe away my sins—
excrement baked onto my flesh like clay.

I did not hear the light sing again
until the day my mother died.

Then it turned electric, turned operatic:
ping, ping, ping went its tiny bells. *Ping, ping, ping.*

Once Mother came
into my room reeking of gin.
I curled deep in the half-
shell of myself waiting for her blows.

Instead, she walked over
to my bed, climbed on top
of me and passed out.
I thought she was dying.
I thought she was drowning me
with her liquor-sodden
breath. Beneath her,

I felt like a blank blur,
a smudge on the face of time,
an unraveling penumbra.
In the bin of halted dreams,
my breath became shorter and
shorter while her drool
trickled across my face as if it were
tears. She was the tearless one—

I cried for her, about her,
in her, but she responded
with moth-eaten words, drunken
slurs that made the whole
house tipsy. Her body
was a boat full of June
snow falling incessantly,
insanely from incumbent clouds.

Deep in the forest, I used
      crayons to color the wounds
            in trees: *to touch a wound*

is to touch God's heart.
        I tried to get lost on purpose
            because I was already a missing

person no one missed. Red,
      green, blue, I colored
          till my crayons were stubs.

I loved the wind-whipped trees.
      I painted my cheeks with the sap
         in their pooled wounds.

Skinflint light shimmied
      through oaks and dogwood: *grow now*
        and be the dark wand

of an earthy tree crowned by
      otherworldly blossoms. I wanted
         to sleep in the turn-tossed canopy

and dream my dream of amnesia,
      but spring told its sad story:
         one must die in order to bloom.

Dead then my lame tongue.
      Dead then my stone hands.
        Dead then my feet, heavy

blocks of blackness. Oh to be
      spirited away from Mother
        who committed a sin

when she had me. I stroked
    sunken soft spots:
        ah, ah, trees sighed

and I embraced them, laced
    with their living blood until
        I became a living girl

whose knotty limbs were
    wind-whipped.
        I learned

to break and break again,
    to make love
        with a graceless God.

In kindergarten I pooped
in my pants. Mother tried

to spank me until I was
spanking clean, but I

was a smelly mess. *Dirty girl,
filthy girl*: was my soul still

clean or did it, too, stink
to high heaven where angels

held their noses when they
smelled me? While I went

away to my cuckoo land,
my name became a dead legend

Mother wanted to forget. I was less
than a wing-bone—*I was shit*—

no more than a thumbtack stuck
in a map of warring countries where

the living walked like the dead
who reeled and reeled—*O*

Mommy love me!—in their
endless drunken stupor that

endlessly stupefied the stink-
pot that was me, me, me.

2 • An Itty Bitty Ditty

Cheep, cheep,
        chirped the birds
                while I echoed back,

cheap. cheap
        because I could be had
                for a nickel or a dime

by any comer or taker—truly
        I could not bear
                to be the empty nest

or the fragile egg.
        Shrieking, clawing went
                the birds, but I could not

move because I was
        a departed feather fallen
                from a prehistoric bird

whose wing span was
        greater than God's embrace.
                This was before mothers

were born. This was
        before my adolescence
                became a stone

in a bird's gullet.
        Stones don't sing,
                stones don't fly.

Ring-a-ding-ding,
        came my ode to being
                a thing meant to endure

till the last raptor folds
     its wings and dives
          into an apocalyptic sea.

Pretty, said Mom
on the night of the prom,
but she meant my shadow
of bone, shadow of shroud,
a net with hooks.
What did I catch?
Boy after boy
who were out to enjoy
sweets for the sweet,
but I was dog meat,
and my body knew the pain
of hammers and saws.
I was a wishbone
utterly broken by boys
who poked and prodded
until my mind boggled
with mish-mash dreams
snagged in my bug-a-boo soul.
I was a voodoo doll
my mother stuck pins in.
Pretty, she said as though
I were a ditty, an itty bitty
ditty not even God would pity.
Ditty gone silent. Ditty
gone numb as a thumb,
ho-hum, ho-hum.

Push them back, push them back,
      I cheered while boys longed
            to snarf me up.

I was an inflatable doll
      that bounced back up
            when the chill wind slapped my cheeks.

I cheered on and on
      beneath a stillborn sky
            darkened by autumn's death pangs.

Oh how I jumped, oh how I smiled:
      I was an A+ girl
            with an A+ aching heart

who yelled, *hold that line, hold*
      that line, as though it were the ending
            in an A+ perfect poem.

While boys milked my breasts until
they were empty, I longed to be donned

in a habit. I wanted to float down cloistered
corridors like a black butterfly whose scales

were relics stolen from Mary. I wanted to marry
a martyr, I wanted to be a saint, but

my lips were rubbed raw by too many kisses
from boys who took and took—suffering would be

my salvation, my one way ticket to a heaven
full of copulating angels—they loved a good fuck

and I dreamed of dreaming in their lascivious arms.
There I would get pregnant with a baby angel

and I would mother her tenderly while my own mother
lay drunk on the sofa, smoking a cigarette

like a tiny flare that signaled her heartbeat.
Soon, soon I would be a centerfold saint

she would kneel before praying a prayer that sounded
like curses—o glory be the day I condemned her

to the hell she belonged in—it was a zoo,
it had a cage and I had the key.

I played piano and sang
for my mother in the rusting light
of late summer days while
green birds preened their feathers
and clicked ebony beaks.

My voice held drops of honey
and the ivory keys were the color
of her tobacco-stained teeth.
I lived in orphaned light
orphaned by an orphaned sun.

My mother snoozed on the gold
couch while I sang about
poor, wayfaring strangers,
a motherless child.

When I was done singing my head
kept ringing in the doleful day.
I rubbed her back: I was
a bluesy girl, a-truly-wanting-
her-mother-very-much-girl,

but she sank into sleep,
dead sleep, rolling upon
melancholy eventide
while I watched over her,
gently, ever so gently.

Dr. Flesh, where were you
        while I was pinned
                by a boy like a broken toy

in the back seat
        cave of his car?
                You could have healed

the scabs on my womb,
        hickies on my neck—
                each tongue was a snake

hissing in my kissy mouth.
        My body knew the burden of birds—
                how to sing when gobs of spit

licked my lips above
        and below: *tweet, tweet,*
                came my incessant refrain.

Dr. Flesh, Dr. Flesh, remember me—
        I was that girl on the homecoming float
                whose crown cracked.

I waved and waved
        to the crowd in the stadium—
                I was too cute for words, especially

the ones *I love you.*

I was nineteen when I took
a razor to my wrists:
cut, cut, cut, cut, slicing
my lifeline in half.
God took and took.
My mother took and took—
where were the violets I hid
in Dixie cups for her to find?
Where was the penny candy
I left in the mailbox
for her to eat?
Nineteen, sent home,
I walked around the lagoon
while my mother stewed
in her boozy brew.
The swans flew
from me like lost love
when I tossed them
chunks of bread.
I wandered in the nearby garden
among headless flowers—
only their thorns were alive,
copper spear tips
meant to go deeply
into my heart.
The sky was an empty
skein of shadow. Cold
walked into me and through me.
Ever penetrating
were invisible knives
while in the visible world
bits of greenery trickled
on trees and tippled
the knotted grasses.
My heart was a fistful of knots.

How do you undo someone who's
already undone?
Stitch the bud back
onto the stem
and water it with your tears,
boo-hoo, boo-hoo.

Grunt, grunt, went each young man
       I let into my cloistered cave,
              a body webbed by shadows

and wings. *Tweet, tweet,* sang my bird-
       like voice. *Meow, meow,* purred my
              sex-kitten soul. *Woof, woof,* went my dog

while the angel of my poverty hovered
       on the ceiling like a faint cartoon.
              On her breast was a tattoo

of the sacred heart—its bubbles of blood
       dripped upon me,
              a torture test.

Was I doomed to be saved?
       Was love more than a creepy crawler feeling?
              I wanted those men to lift

my featherweight soul out of my feather-
weight body till passion
       preyed and prayed upon it.

In my head I sang an elegy
       to that famished angel. *Pant, pant,* went my dog.
              He loved me more than I did.

Whiskey, I downed whiskey
and my whiskey dreams
whisked me out of my body.
My lips were stitched closed,
my wing buds sliced

till my brain turned into
a boob tube all fuzzy
with broken snow that fell
in the pell-mell hell of
silent, flightless birds.

I was the girl who burned
and burned in the city
of her brains. I drank to sink
beneath Mother's dead-lead words:
exit in order to exist

while a meager bird fluttered
in my meager soul and my body
was a wrecked vessel pulled
under by the undertow of
an underworld lusting for me
as though I were Persephone.

Mother would not grieve my loss,
would not make the world barren
because she was the Baroness of all
that's barren: *dead-bed,*
dead-head, dead-red-blood.

I wanted to be whittled away like the empty whistle the wind
whines through.

Barely, scarcely grown, I was a crybaby who cried along with
the sick shadows

that sagged in my body. I wanted to eat the blue stars high above
my building

where a woman was shot dead in the head.
I knew

what it was like to be dead in the head—in my dreams
I glided

down rows of headstones, a nubile bride.
Without

my many lonely sorrows—they were my succor, my *crème
de la crème*—

I would have disappeared in thin wind which, like a small
tornado,

had a doll-like eye that never blinked, never winked.
Rather it cried

along with my crybaby tears shed by a barely there woman
dying to die.

Twenty, pregnant, I stood
before the triptych of my windows,
gazing at an oak
that looked fatherly:
o hold me in your infallible limbs.
I was a lonely vigil and my womb
held a collapsed flame.
I could tell no one.
I could not bear this child
because I could not bear myself.
Dust within a dust baby,
I lay on my bed and placed
my hands on my belly
as if I could pray
this little bit of a being
out of my womb.
Go away, I cried,
but the purple poodles
on my wallpaper
foamed at the mouth—
hungry, hungry, hungry,
were these rabid dogs
while I longed for a killing frost
to kill what was inside me.
When the room rocked
and changed sizes,
I chanted a cracked
litany and rosary beads
knotted in my heart.
I was twenty. I could not bear
to be alive while there grew in me
a bruised bud I could not
let open, so I closed myself
in a coma that stunned both me
and my little slip of a thing
into silence
only God, who never came near,
could hear.

3 • Tra-la-la

Busy being a dust-baby blown
  this way and that
    like a swarm of gnats,

I shattered into stinging particles.
  It was my son's eleventh birthday
    and I would not, could not come back—

then, suddenly, I became a woman
  wrestling with God in an abyss
    closed shut with a sewer lid—

limb upon limb, we pinned
  each other in sewage.
    My husband took me

to the hospital. When I
  stepped out of the car, I sang,
    "tra-la-la," as if I were

Cinderella going to an enchanted ball.
  Was my son blowing out
    the candles on his birthday cake?

Should I sing the birthday song
  even though I wasn't there?
    And where, exactly, was I?

I stuffed my mouth with toilet paper
  so I wouldn't start to scream,
    so my dust-baby wouldn't be blown

to smithereens, so I could finally pin
  down God in piss and shit till
    he cried *monkey.*

In the psych ward, I remained
a dust-baby. One breath
would blow me into the four corners
of the wind. I clutched

my baby picture and my son's
favorite teddy bear. Lions
walked out of walls. Howler monkeys
screamed their cries of grief.

It was all wave and wavering.
I watched the river from my window—
it was the color of mother-of-pearl
and the snow died in it.

I fell to my knees while remembering
how much my mother loved
the dogwood blossoms:
each was a pink velvet boat.

I was ready to be castaway,
but in what dark harbor
would I be utterly human
which is to say, hardly begun?

Soon after my arrival in my
above-ground underworld, Dr. Flesh
put me on display
for a game of Show and Tell.
I was to tell the dark glory
of my hunky-dory story
to a group of students
who wanted to be
just like Dr. Flesh
who was special,
very, very special
unlike me.
I perched on a stool that
belonged in a barroom
and started to use my words.
I was a talking tree
and my leaves were on fire.
Where was the fire engine,
the whine of sirens
on the way to put out smoke
I exuded like plumes of fumes?
I talked about the seizures,
hundreds of seizures I had
for seemingly hundreds of years.
I jerked up and down
and all the way around
flat on my back on the floor.
One time, my son, then seven
or eight, fed me meds
and read "The Stinky Cheese Man"
while I flayed this way and that
as if to fend off Mother.
The body remembers everything
while the breath, sweet breath
longs to escape us.

I couldn't escape Mother—
she chased me down the hallway,
the long, long hallway
like a primitive predator
while I screamed and screamed.
No one heard me,
nor alas, did you, Dr. Flesh.
I saw you yawn as I went on—
like a dying fly
flinging itself
against the pane that holds
her in.

It was almost Christmas. I hoarded quarters
to make calls out. When I spoke to my son,

my words were full of hollow sounds that came
from the hollow wisdom of dead Mother:

carve out what's inside until a certain
weightlessness tells you it's time to die.

Wearing my flannel nightgown, I stood by
the windows in my room. I wanted to leap

out that window just to feel the beauty
of falling in breathtaking air. Instead,

I looked into another hospital window in
another ward. Night after night, an old

woman massaged the back of an even
older man under the stern glow of the ceiling light.

I wished them the respite deep within
the silent hearts of snowflakes then falling

like hordes of tiny white butterflies,
but more than that I wanted to be back

in the maternity ward where I had given birth
to my son eleven winters before. It was a snowy

December twilight when he began to crown.
I pushed and pushed as if squeezing my portion

of heaven out of my body. My husband held
my hand. In between contractions I snoozed

and he thought I was dying. Perhaps I was.
Perhaps the fruitful one would replace the fruitless

fig of the woman I was. The lights were dimmed.
My husband's shadow was a benevolent God.

In one big gush, my son came out.
He was brought to my breast. He latched on

and became fully alive to a mother who now stood
before suicide-proof windows watching the river

move like a black snake flickering thousands of
venomous tongues that poisoned a charred, scarred sky.

The timeless air I breathed
was shrapnel and I was a mess
of flesh. I was told I could die
from drinking too much water
so I drank cup after cup
after cup.

When my husband visited
there wasn't much of a me
to see. He kissed my forehead
as if it were a door to a chapel
wherein the holy ululations
of lamentation were heard
morning, noon and night.

I was a boneless tree in a
toneless forest. I was half past
dead among the demented
as Mother had been when she
lived. And when she died

she turned into an inky fluid
that drained in my veins
which the crows plucked to line
empty nests in the blue-black
fright of native night.

In Arts and Crafts,
I cooked up things
to make for my son.
In this overnight camp
for the crazed,
our twitchy fingers
and even twitchier minds
needed something to do.

One day we made a mural
for the coming holiday season.
A very fine painter—deluded,
depressed—painted with
panache and finesse
the coal-black eyes of
the snowman he was becoming.
When we hung it in the TV room,
everyone applauded.

I made a journal for my son,
glued fabric to the cover
of an old composition book,
pasted on inspiring sayings
cut from magazines:
*our greatest glory is not
in falling but in RISING UP
every time we fall,*
Emerson wrote,
but what did he know
about falling and falling
like a bouncing ball
down the cellar stairs?

My son did not know
where I was.
I had to take tests
like the five-hundred

question survey I took upon arrival.
Do you like golf? it asked
and when I wrote "no"
I was diagnosed.

On the front of the journal,
I pasted a picture of a skier at sunset—
roseate colors cut through
the snow the skier cut through—
whatever you do, or dream you can,
begin it now. Boldness has genius
power and magic in it:
BEGIN IT NOW,
Goethe wrote, but I
could begin nothing but
my itty bitty deaths.

Huff-huff, choo-choo
came my breath which grew
shorter and shorter, knowing
there was no one at home
to bake the Christmas cookies
or read "The Grinch Who Stole Christmas."
I was a grinch
stuck in my little getaway.
O dear boy,
remember me sadly.

I was exotic, chaotic, a riot in the aerobics class I went to
every day.

I wore designer clothes with hospital socks, moved
in rhythm

to the beat—*and 1 and 2 and 3 and 4*—while counting in time with
my ticking heart,

which was winding down like an abandoned merry-go-round.
A prima donna,

I turned round and round, shimmied my hips, hopped from
foot-to-foot.

We were a groovy gang and for a purebred moment I felt
joy

like a flame that leapt out of the burning pits of Dante's inferno.
This flame

danced while I stretched from side-to-side. I fit
right in

with the clique—fruitcakes! nutcases!—just like me.
Counting

the beats, I tried to plug up my bleeding soul by laughing out loud:
ha-ha, ha-ha.

Named insane, named suicidal, I was the ghost
of God's body and there was a gorgeous vowel deep

in my heart of hearts. How to sound it in my
 gilded throat?
It was a lover's sigh, a musical note in love

with itself and the sound of light in creamy clouds.
O what a scanty thing I was in that winter

of winters when hell-bent angels wanted to mate
with me, but I was an absentee and dreams

lunged out of me like rabid dogs and my scent—
burnt match, cursed cinder—trailed me

like a smoky mood. I abandoned myself
in the unit where there were no sharps, where

there were no cords, where I was checked
every ten minutes and my pulse was stolen.

When I came out of the unit,
the world, I noticed, had grown
more expansive, more expressive:
even the air tingled. The light

was bolder with a big voice—*stir*
in the liqueur of my syrup—which could be
shared, like blood between kin.
The clouds were no longer sharks

and the silence had a beautiful whir beneath
its shining template. *Where were you?*
people would ask. No one wanted to hear,
I was in the lockup, the loony bin.

It was there where my lifeless
life began as something
gone asunder: there was thunder
in the far side of my brain, burrs
snared in my veins, my heart,
a collapsed parachute.

After falling and falling for days on end,
I had finally hit ground, but
I could not yet walk upon it because
my footprints were scars on papyrus.

I was the blistered thorn in God's side,
the cloudiness inside a child's favorite
marble, and when my son ran into my arms
to greet me, I swung him so high
I thought he might forgive me.

4 • O Healing Go Deep

Just now stunted autumn
      stunts me: the raked leaves
            of my childhood burn

and I breathe in slashed ribbons
      of smoke. *Feast on ashes,*
            feast on ashes—I crumble

into crumbs the crows—manic,
      shrieking—descend upon, forever
            a doll with crooked limbs

folded in a crooked loneliness:
      hollow stalk, hollow stone,
            hollow egg—so

much dying one must do
      in order to be stung alive.
            O mercy be wild, o healing go deep.

The rivulets of bruised blood which trickled from
my wrists

when I was nineteen still flow in me like
hot, black tar.

The scars are tiny railway tracks: *choo-choo*,
I chuff away

while the conductor tips his hat, winks at me
lascivious.

At home, Mother yelled at me while I became
an elderly doll

carved out of a chunk of ice from the world's oldest
iceberg.

Clink, clink, went the cubes in her drink while deep
in the dark

of my room, I pressed my tongue against the frozen
windowpane

until it was scorched by frost flowers I dare to bear
like scars.

The sky is punched by those
who raise their fists and yell,
enough, enough.
I am one of them—
enough I say of my careening
craziness, of being
a thing in thin wind
running away from Mother.
I was a broken arc on a broken sea
which sang, *sink to be saved,*
sink to be saved.
Why oh why did she
thunder my head with the bat?
Was it because I sucked my thumb,
tried to break into her candy safe,
longed to be a Little Princess
in a party dress and sparkly shoes?
Instead, my secondhand body
dressed in secondhand clothes,
turned into a mannequin
in *rigor mortis.* Once,
she said, we're all
victims of victims,
but she was a savage scavenger
like lions and tigers and bears,
oh no, oh no.

I'm yanked into fits
      of madness like a hanky
            out of a magician's pocket.

Under spotlights as big as God's eyes,
      I'm that scantily
            dressed woman outlined

by knives while I'm sawed
      in half in my own coffin.
            A voiceless dove still sings:

the circuit of wounds is a necklace
      of star flowers. One by one,
            they burst open—*pop,*

pop, pop, like a toy gun
      and their green blood floods
            the world with a green energy

feeding a feast of seeds.
      Pop, pop, pop, goes my heart when
            my husband kisses me on the forehead

after finding me hiding in the closet,
      a sick doll whose pupils
            are black moons, whose veins

trickle with flowery blood, ounce
      by ounce, until I want to go
            into the wise ways death knows about,

but keeps secret, like the
      magician's best trick—
            open my coffin and see the dead

walk again: *hip-hop, bip-bop.*

Autumn's feathery weather wends me apart:
be the dark ping of a thing, be the drop

of spit on God's lips. Furthering furtively goes
my heart, which fits in a hole of empty air. If only

I could blow apart the room of my childhood
where my bed was a tomb where in tears and fears,

I grew old as the moon which stopped, a dead clock.
Tick-tock, tick-tock, goes the flowers whose spines

are weakening, whose blooms are butter drowning
in autumn's weary light. Can you spare me a dime

to put in a slit in time? Can the living
divorce the dead? *Hell's bells,* it's time.

If my mother dared to come near
me now, I would nail her hands together
until they looked folded in prayer.
She would not beg for forgiveness,

but there in the old forest, my husband
down on his knees, touches
the green tips of the baby hemlocks
as though they were turgid nipples.

He knows to live in this world
means loving all that's ripening
for death—a prison sentence
for the doll I once was

who cried her way, blood
by blood cell, into being more
than a dead body, outlined in chalk-
dust the spring rain, with its

hail of seed, could wash away.

My demons came inside the house
to attack with their black and red

scaled reptilian wings, a nightmare
of chimera. They flew low, screeching,

and I screamed so loud my husband
could hear me on the street.

He found me in a ball, fed me
meds, but still, demons lit upon me

full throttle. They pushed me into a shell
and I tumbled, head down in death's canal.

Wordless, hell was wordless and I
was in it. Eyes closed tight, I was a great

ocean falling apart. My bones snared in
sticky webs, my flesh as well. Winter's ghost

flew into me and my soul loosened
like an eye from its socket. *Elizabeth,*

Elizabeth, came my husband's voice.
Was that my name? *Elizabeth, Elizabeth.*

Wing and wavelength, breath surrounding
a star tree. *Elizabeth, Elizabeth.*

A foster self slowly came round, woke
to the world and cried, *bye-bye, bye-bye.*

I want to garden in this January rain
       as if to do so would redeem
              the flowers that redeem me.

I bow before the winter garden
       because every arousal is an act of love.
          How to arouse the one

sucked out of me like red, wet pearls?
       Who will put flesh on her sore bones,
          lure her into listening to

the murmuring rain? I'm schooled
       by the garden's earthy lessons:
          to blossom is to be manic, to die

is to become a bleeding absence.
       Today nature bares its bruised breast
          full of damaged seed, as do I

to an earth resting up for death.

This is what I sing: *there's a hole*
in my head, drear mother, drear mother

while I become an orphan of the girl
I once was. She's a paltry twig, a sliver

of sky's blue ribbons, lost drop of
in a waterfall that surges with the energy

of torrential sunlight and the cocoon
the tornado spins in. My orphanage

is temple, shack, or roadside attraction
where I am a bizarre abbreviation

of what it is to be, which means
one who cups the shattered flower of her heart

tenderly while standing in God's shadow.
He worships the broken ones: a stripper with breast cancer,

grieving clown and beautiful suicidal girls.
Step up, I say, to the ruined attic and listen

to the picture of the boy or girl you were
for it is a poem unleashing its avowals

that keep us wedded to the buried one
we carry in a satchel of torn-up dreams.

Where is the leash of light
I can cling to in order
to be brought back from
the burnt brink

to an ordinary world
where I would be cooking
an ordinary supper for
my husband and son?

When they sit down
at the kitchen table, I
suddenly begin to ward off
lions and tigers and bears

oh no, with a chair.
They tell me there are no
lions and tigers and bears.
They tell me to come back, but

they may as well be asking
what the dust wants to be.
Supper grows cold while
the meds kick in. When

that happens we become
an ordinary family eating
ordinary food, but I'm
feeding those beasts—

oh no, oh no—who will
eat me as if sucking
an egg out of a pinhole
in its hollow blue shell.

Mother hit me again and again:
I was the wordless one, but I am

speaking now: we are flesh upon bone,
mortal and broken. This, too: there is

a heaven inside hell and a hell inside heaven
and I have been in both. I know how

Mother came to be: she was a dragon's tooth
planted in cracked earth till she sprang up,

a soldier hungry for slaughter. Her sword
split the hairs on my head, her copper spear tip

is a bruised thorn in my womb. I was
a flammable angel she dragged

through flaming doors: the stench of burnt
flesh sticks to me like sweat. Rip-shit,

Mother was rip-shit and now that she
is dead I shiver alive in a world ghosted

by a god who abandoned himself
on a crucifix of stark bones.

Reptilian demons once attacked me
    while I curled in a tight ball
        on the floor and screamed

until the Sisters of Solace came
    to console me. *Speak now,*
        they said, *and your words*

will be more than adornments.
    How does one turn a human cry
        into a living word? All my life,

I have lived in the origin
    of original wounds, which is
        to say, God's body.

No one can break his bones,
    but his heart, dear heart,
        clots with snow while birth-

pangs, death pangs entwine him
    like a vine that chokes
        the living tree

until I speak given words:
    be alive enough to dream
        your way into redemption.

When Mother was
alive, she trained fire
to lick my feet, but now
she wears the death mask,
the heavy death mask
while I'm masked by fits
of madness quick
as a lightning bolt—
she trained fire—
that goes directly
into my mind's eye. Banished

into breakage I do what I
I don't want to do—
one day found me trying
to crawl inside the dog's
crate, another found me
under the vanity
having a tea party with
my dolls while drinking
from Mother's baby cup.

I made a toast
to my stellar hell,
the condemned cathedral
of my childhood home
where I envied the crucifixes
in every room because no one
prayed to me and I, too,
longed for resurrection.

While my words become blooming elegies,
God pries me open like a clam shell

full of snot and pearls, snot and pearls.
My heart is a sweet tooth addicted

to darkness, the frightening dark full of
scabs and scales. Who will bring me back

when I disappear in the hidey-hole
of my brain with a voice that says:

touch-me-not, love-me-not? This
is when my name breaks down into

bitter dust tumbling like a tumbleweed
in catacombs of the dead. There

my mother greets me with a teeny-
weenie kiss that blisters my lips.

Go in to go under, go in to plunder
was the motto of her blankedy-blank

life. O tour-de-force of living tears—
what holds me together? Cord of water?

Slipknot of air? Downward motion
has no magic potion and there's sparkly stuff

in my head letting out thousands of tiny
shocks. In the cave of my childhood,

I made a little music: *mouse-music,*
mouse-music and once the sound of a cricket

buried in flames. The Kyrie of its cry
never retires, nor do I. I was

a grey-haired child, had a wizened
face, bones full of hot wires.

Damage is done when love is undone
and I'm a bouquet of burnt matches,

an ashen petal fallen from a loony-
tunes moon. Stomp, smudge, chalk

me into cinders and I will rise like
a genie out of a bottle of destitute dreams.

My scent is offal, seared grass
and dirt drenched with the blood of

the war dead. Why must there be
warring between heaven and earth,

dead Mother and me? The kiss of peace
has been smeared into blear

and white doves have bloodied their feathers
in hell's red bile of dew. I can be scraped

from the bottom of God's shoe, my scars
are pregnant with pain and I am a bloody stew.

Dressed in mole's clothes, I dig
past my open grave with raggedy paws

till I'm blinded with blinding light
that scorches the blackened wick

of my blackened soul, my masterpiece.

Design and Production

Cover and text design by Kathy Boykowycz
Cover painting, "Satin Doll," by Sirarpi
Heghinian Walzer

Text set in Adobe Garamond, designed in
1989 by Robert Slimbach from the original
16-century fonts
Headings set in ITC Bradley Hand, designed
in 1995 by Richard Bradley

Printed by Thomson-Shore of Dexter, Michigan,
on Nature's Natural, a 50% recycled paper